GRADE 1
THINKING SKILLS

Fun-filled Activities

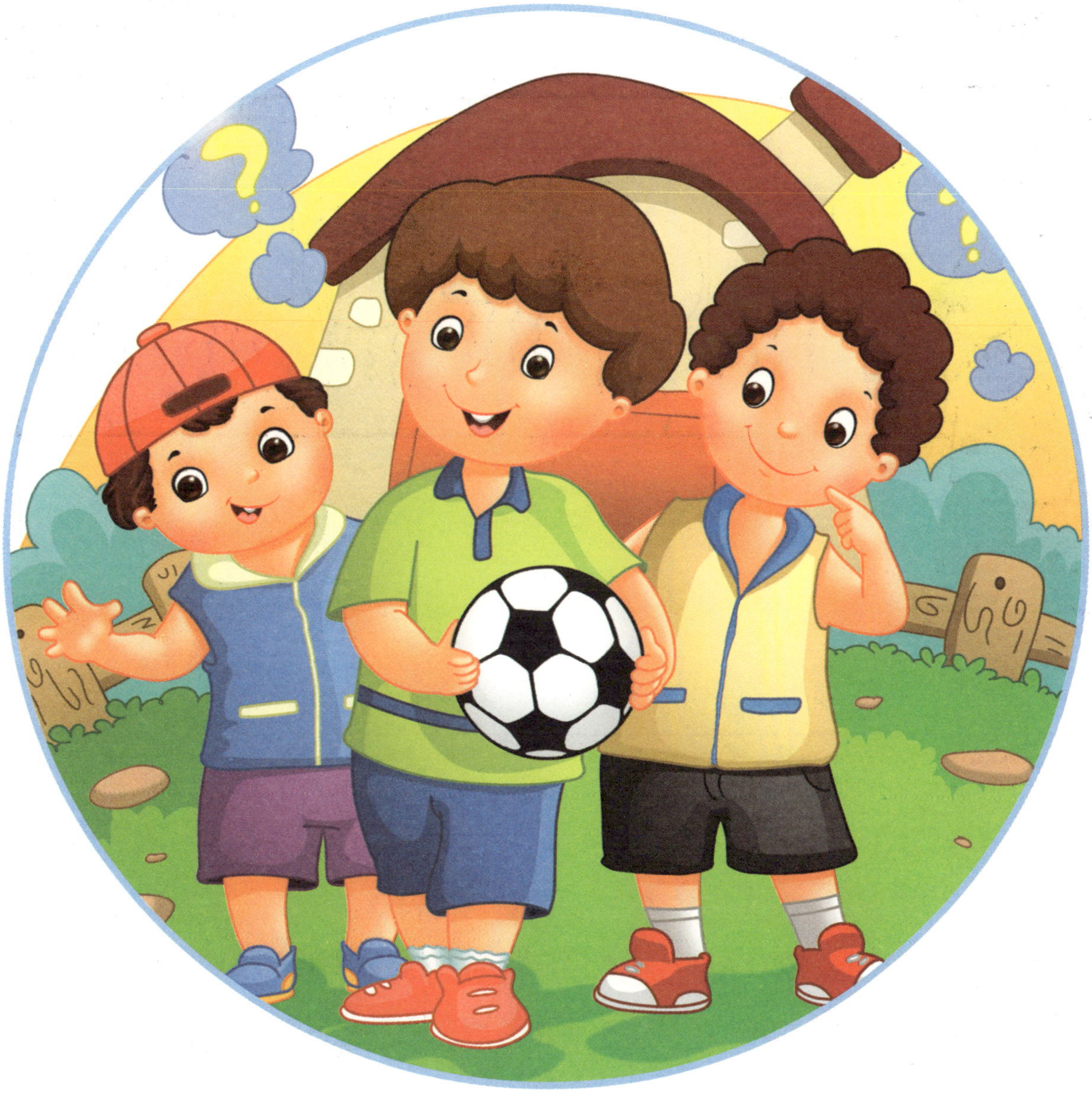

Om KIDZ
An imprint of Om Books International

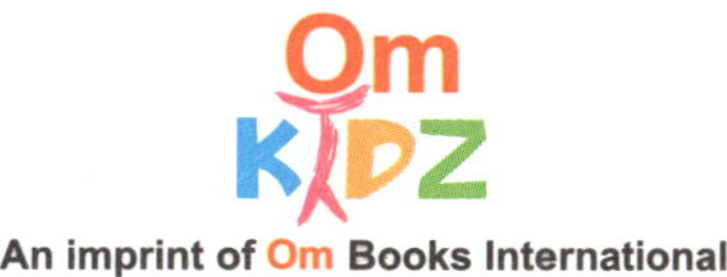

Let's Guess the Colour!

Tiddy is happy to paint the wall. Read the clues for him and guess which colour is each shape.

Colour the shapes.

Clues

- Red is not next to brown.
- Green is not a square.
- Yellow is between white and green.
- Pink is to the left of brown.

At the Birthday Party!

Maria, Ben, Andy and John are at John's birthday party.

Draw lines on the cake so that each child gets equal piece. How many lines do you need to draw?

Pattern Balloons!

Addie painted balloons with patterns. She made two of each. Can you find the pairs of balloons with the matching pattern?

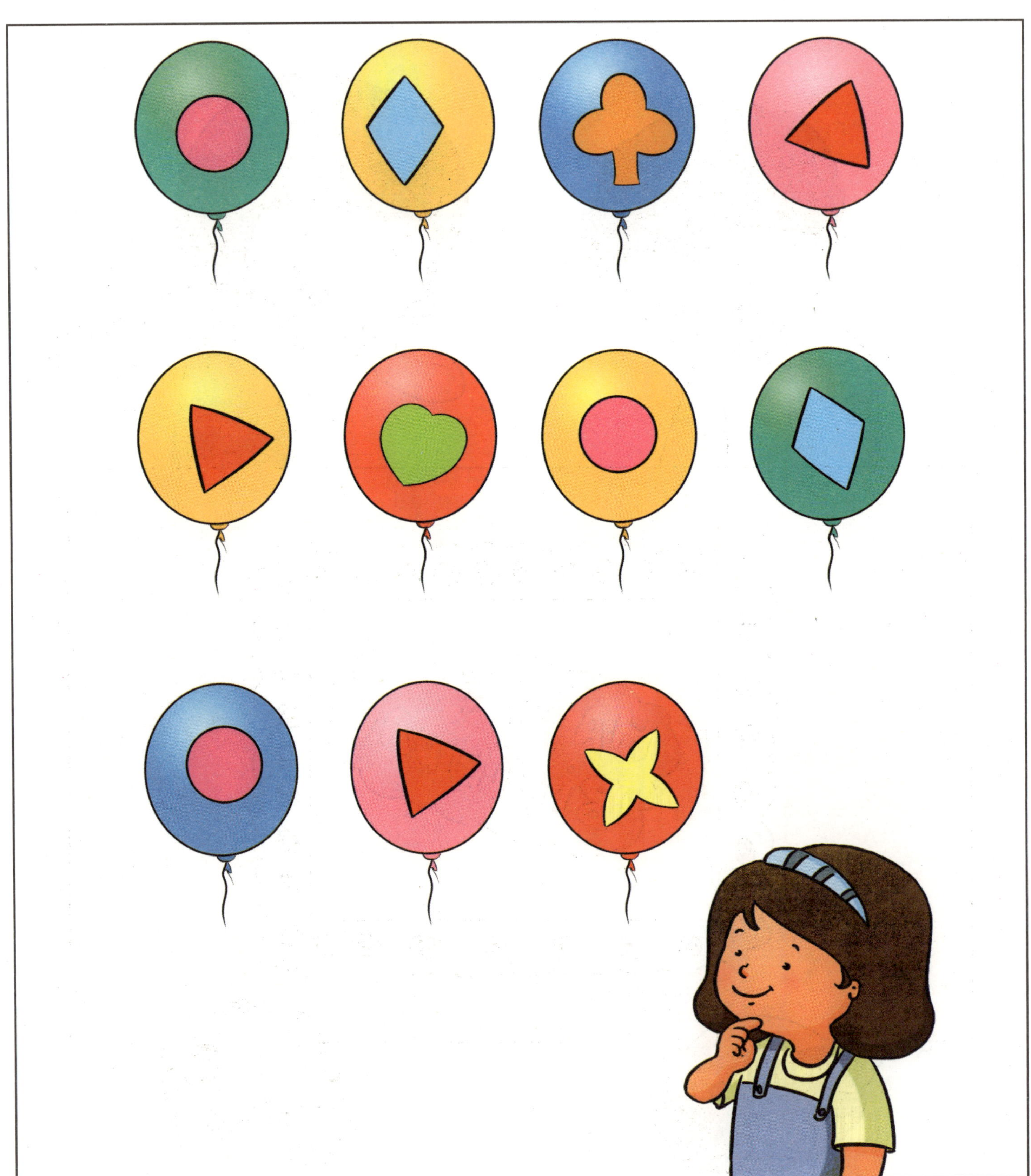

The Missing Piece!

Mr. Mac has made a delicious pizza. But a mouse has picked a piece from it! Can you find the piece that will fit into the missing spot?

Fly High!

The children are flying kites.

Use these clues to colour the kites flying high.

1. The biggest kite is yellow.
2. The blue kite is not the last one.
3. The orange kite is between the yellow and blue one.
4. One kite is purple.
5. The smallest kite is red.

Design My Quilt!

Mama Bear is making a quilt for the Baby Bear. Can you complete the pattern that she has started?

Crunchy Cookie Pattern

Winny is making tray arrangements for the guests. Help her complete the crunchy cookie pattern on the tray.

Now, complete the patterns given below.

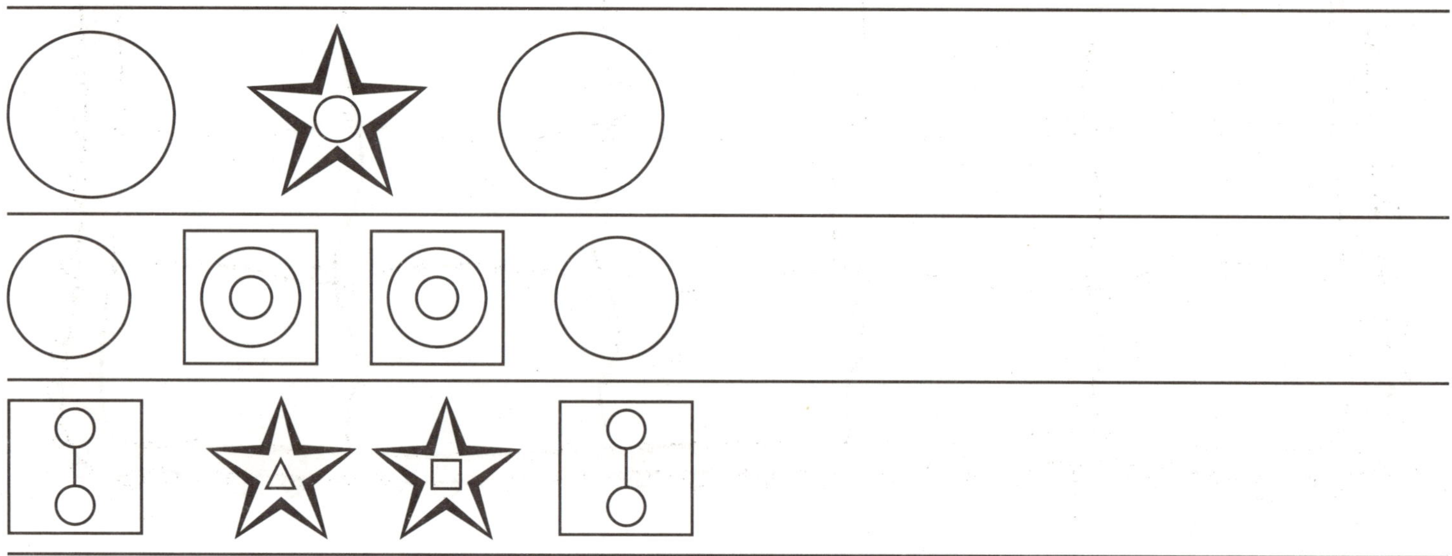

Easter Eggs!

The Bunny is making a pattern on the Easter eggs. Can you complete the pattern to help him?

It's time to make your own Easter eggs with interesting patterns. Get, set, go!

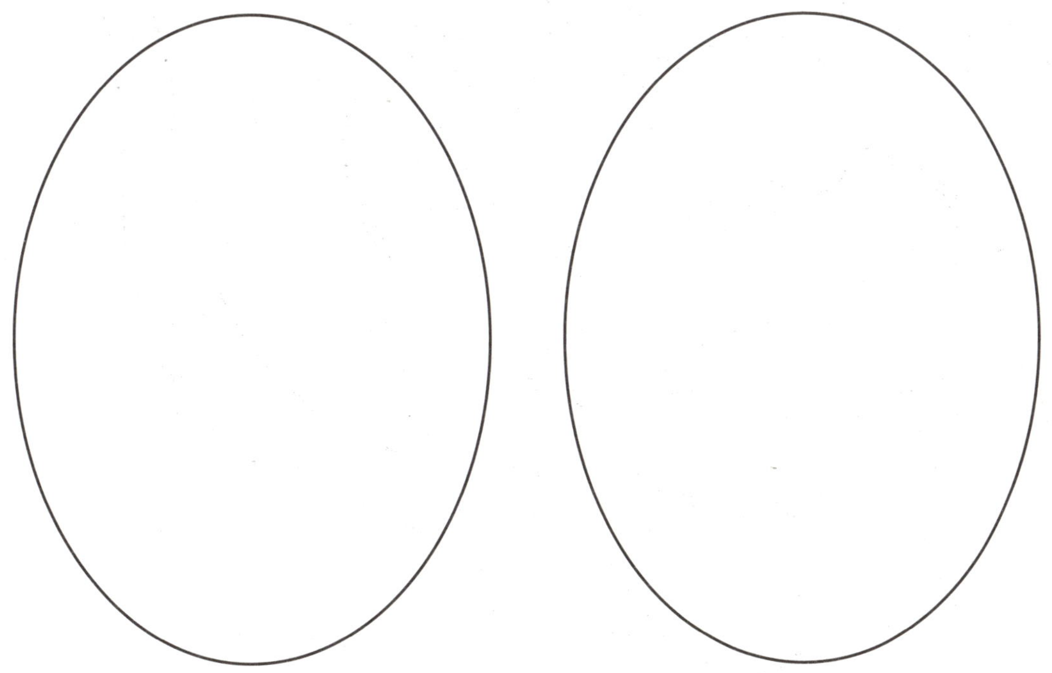

Catch the Fly!

The frog can catch the fly if he hops from one lily pad to another just four times. He can only hop on the lily pads connected by a line. Help him catch the fly by drawing hops. How many ways did you find?

Back Home!

Puff is off for a walk! Help him return home from where it started.
You can visit only 20 points and all the 3 circles.

Fun on the Rides!

Find and circle the hidden pictures.

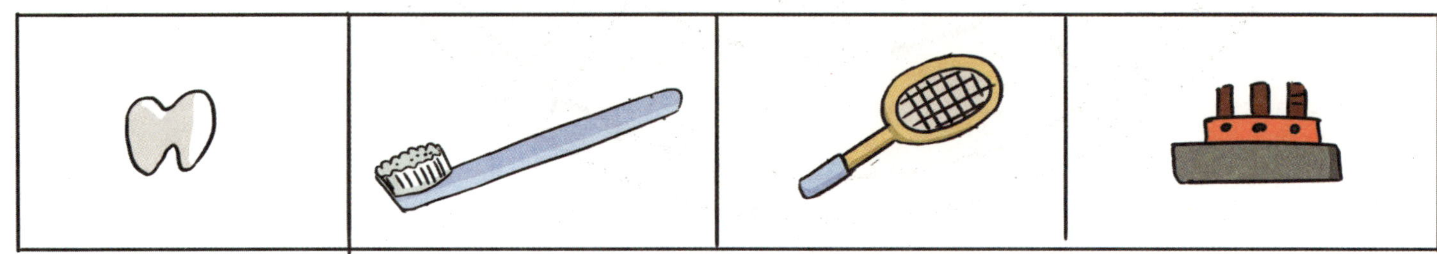

It's Fun to Read!

Find and circle the hidden pictures.

It's Buggy's Birthday!

Buggy has got a gift from his friend. It has the name of the month he was born in. Draw a line to divide the strange symbols on the pot and find it.

Let's try more!

Draw lines to divide these symbols to decode the words.

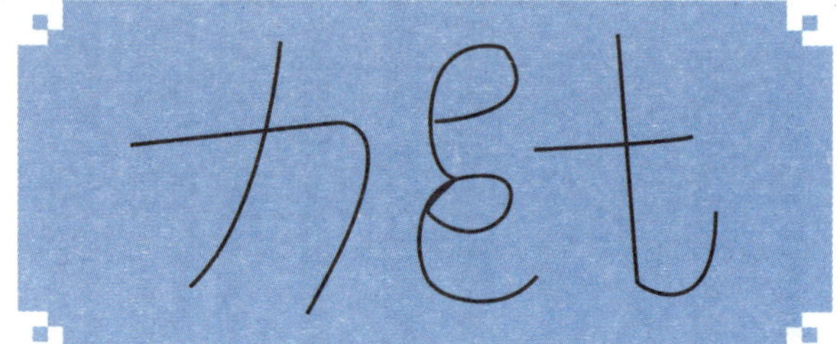

Three Squares!

Doopy the duck wants to draw these squares. Help him draw this pattern in one continuous line so that you don't lift the pencil point off the paper.

Try and make these patterns without lifting your pencil point.

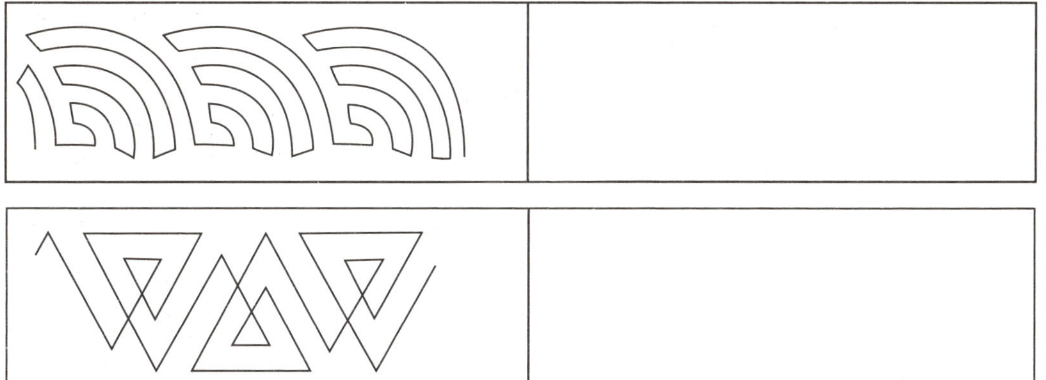

It's Time to Climb!

Tim wants to climb the blocks. Help him reach the top by following the given colour code:

• green • yellow • red • blue.

Move the Bars!

Pete the pirate is piling his gold bars. He wants to make all the piles of the same height. He can just make three moves. Circle the bars and draw arrows to indicate it.

Help Me Reach the Nuts

Squitter, the squirrel has discovered a map for his buried nuts. It says:

Follow the number that is greater than the one you are on. Can you help him reach there?

Next Door Neighbours!

Polly has some number cards. Arrange the numbers for him in such a way that any two consecutive numbers are next to each other down and across.

Let's Make a Total!

The bunny is collecting carrots for dinner. How many carrots should the bunny put in the circles such that each line adds up to 16?

Six Pin Bowling

Which pins must James knock down to score exactly 7? Tick the correct pins.

Choose and draw pins from above and find 2 different ways:

to score 8

to score 5

Roll the Dice!

You are playing snakes and ladders and your peg is on 2. You roll the dice and land on 14.

What are the different ways to reach there? Tick the box with the correct dice.

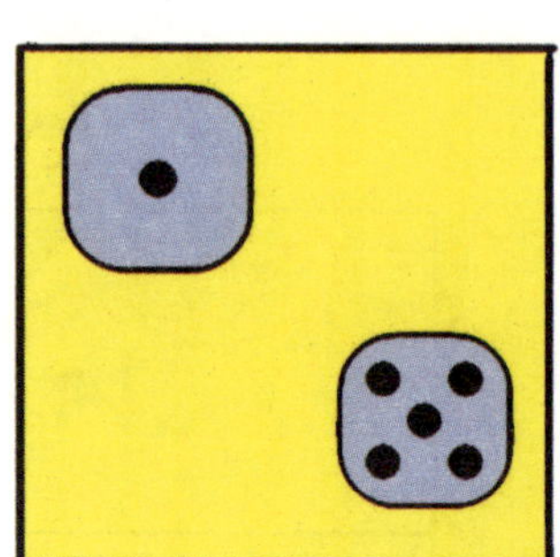

Meet the Magical Triangles!

Place all the numbers from 1 to 6 in the circles along the sides of the triangle so that 3 numbers on each side add up to 12.

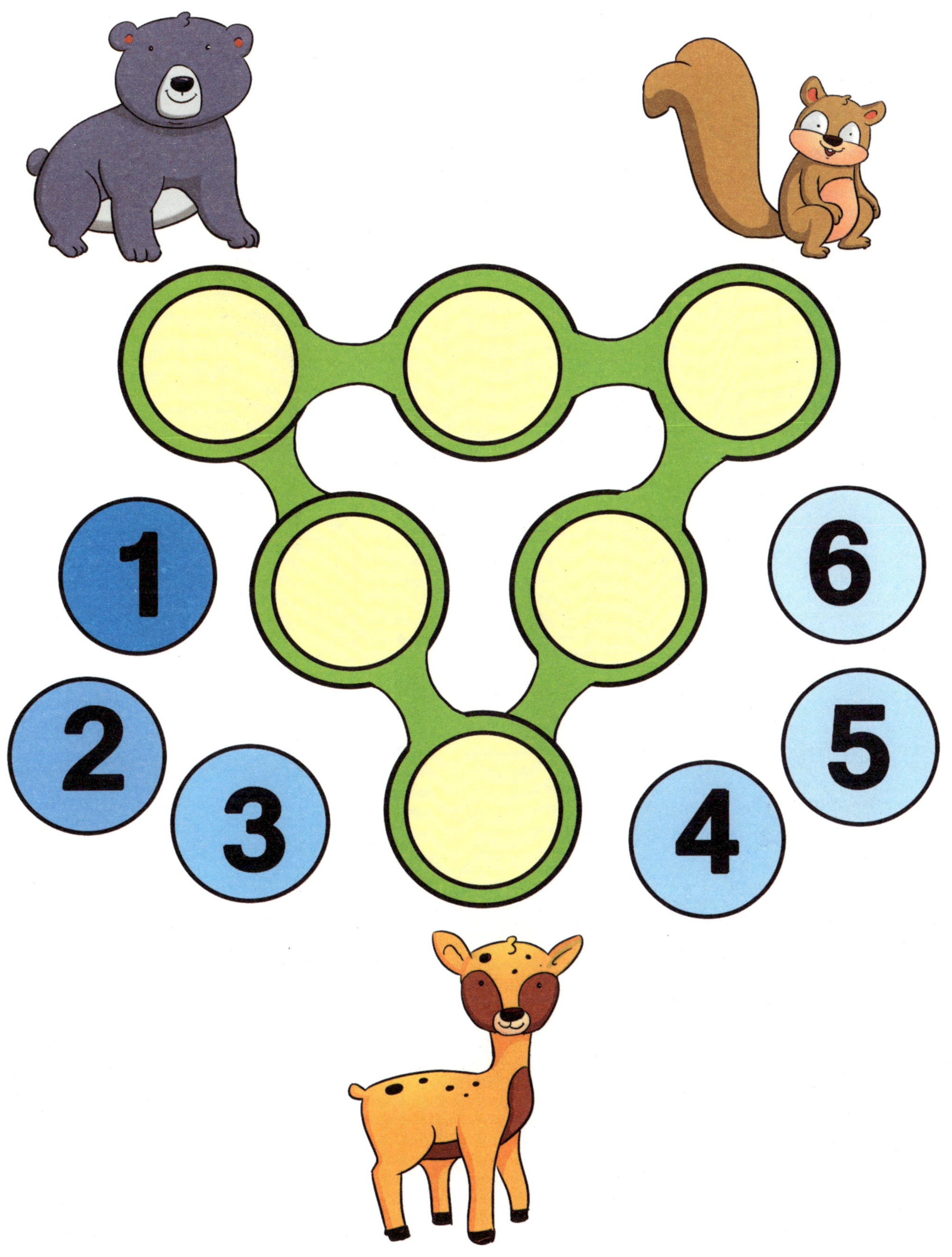

Fireworks Totals!

Elina had some firecrackers. When she burst them, some made 3 stars and some 4. How many stars should you draw in the fireworks so that all make 21?

Who is the Fourth One?

Gini's mother has four children.

The name of the first child is April.

The second one is May.

The name of the third one is June.

What is the name of the fourth child?

____

Who is First in the Queue?

Sam, Polly, Alicia and Sandy went to see a match. Who is standing first in the queue?

Use the clues to find it.

Clues:

The first in the queue is a boy.

Alicia is wearing spectacles.

Sandy is between Sam and Tom.

Sam is not wearing shorts.

Gifts for Us!

Aunt Jane has bought gifts for the children. Read the clues and match the gift boxes to the child it belongs.

1. Max gets the gift just below James'.
2. Linda's gift has stars on it.
3. James' gift is different from everyone's gift.
4. Daniel's gift is long and thin.
5. Neo's gift is behind all gifts.

Which One is Rosh's Dog?

Rosh's dog is lost! Help him find his dog with these clues.

1. Its tail is long.
2. It has short legs.
3. It is without spots.
4. Its ears look like its tail.

Who is David?

We are looking for David. Use these clues and find him. Draw a circle around him.

1. David is happy.
2. David does not play football.
3. David does not have brown hair.
4. David likes to skate.

Your Puzzle!

This page is all yours! Make your own puzzle with letters, shapes and numbers below. Ask your friend to solve it.

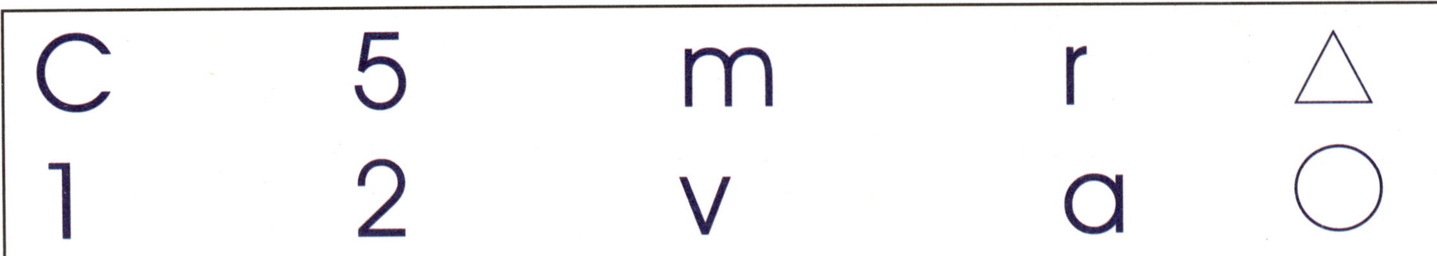

Answer Key

Page 2

Page 3

Page 4

Page 5

Page 6

Page 7

CHILDREN WILL DO ON THEIR OWN.

Page 8

CHILDREN WILL DO ON THEIR OWN.

Page 9

CHILDREN WILL DO ON THEIR OWN.

Page 10

Page 11

CHILDREN WILL DO ON THEIR OWN.

Page 12

Page 13

Page 14

Page 15

CHILDREN WILL DO ON THEIR OWN.

Page 16

Page 17

11	10
6	14
5	13
4	12
3	9
2	8
1	7

Page 18

Page 19

CHILDREN WILL DO ON THEIR OWN.

Page 20

Page 21

CHILDREN WILL DO ON THEIR OWN.

Page 22

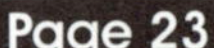

Answer Key

Page 23

Page 24

Page 25

THE FOURTH CHILD IS GINI.

Page 26

SAM, SANDY, TOM, ALICIA

Page 27

Page 28

Page 29

Page 30

CHILDREN WILL DO ON THEIR OWN